I CAN'T HIDE IT

WRITTEN BY: AMANDA JONES

Smileyjonesbooks.info

TABLE OF CONTENTS

<REAL LFE CONTEMPORARY STORIE>

I CAN'T HIDE IT

Whatever you are going through, there is no need to hold it in. Let it go and let God because I Can't Hide It.

NO ONE WOULD LISTEN

She went everywhere for help, and no would could or would help her. She talks with plenty and she said No One Would Listen.

Dedications to:

My Family,

My Friends,

My Church Family,

Special Thank You To

Eric Roach.

I love you all.

I CAN'T HIDE IT

I fell that you are becoming a stranger to. I'm losing my memory of you, feelings of sadness completely believable blue. You seemly distant in my mind, and I'm wondering if you think I'm blind, because I ask God to help me because I'm running out of time. I can't love myself that way anymore it's like a fantasy when I'm stiff like a board. My writings come to me as I think, and the feelings are filled up like a bank. I got a piece of paper and began to write, no more crying in this lullaby.

THE OPENING

As I listen to the preacher my mind wonder in and out from guilt to not guilty. I review my past life as, I review what could be of the future. I have asked for forgiveness and I end up doing the same thing over and over again. I'm going through so much that I can't bear to go through any longer. I have accepted the fact that I need a lot of help spiritually. I don't know what to do, where to turn, and who to turn to. So now I've realize what to do, where to turn, and who to turn to.

It's God!!

I CAN'T HIDE IT

Good Morning! Are you working hard? I hope your day goes well and take it easy. Are you listening to me are you busy as always? Ok. Well I guess I'll talk to you later and I love you.

Sending a text released my feelings and thoughts, which was mainly a cry that was bought. Is it a cry for help, or just to be heard, or getting it off my chest with the word? As long as I sent that text I knew right then I was heard and I was through. Even though most of the time the person didn't respond back, it was ok with me because it was off my rack.

Sometime I even forget what the world I text, just because it wasn't on my mind you just don't know what to expect. My main type of communication was a simple text, and I would do it all day just to see what was next. I'm really about to text now because I got and even greater problem but how, the shock in my life was about to bow, a report big as a cow, of what was found in my house.

My greatest fall was when I found a toxic mold in my house and my kids and I was force to move out. I read the report that was sent to me via email, from the Environmental Consultant saying what he found bewares. The name (Stacybotrus) never cross my mind, I drop my head and thought we would be fine. I try to continue to read. The price to fix would exceed, the cost to remediate my home in deed cost $5,000.00 could you believe. Dropping my head in despair, $18,000.00 is a lot of money to repair. It was too much for me to bear; I move my family out of there.

I call the insurance company which they said it wasn't covered on my policy. I knew something was wrong because my kids and I was back in forwards to the doctor for Asthma, Rhinitis, Bronchitis, Pneumonia, Allergies, Colds, Sinus, and the list goes on. We went to the doctor to get treated for months and months. I ended up on high blood pressure pills. God I thought I need a will. We moved out of the house on May 30, 2011. I know everyone got to die from something, but I wasn't going to let my house kill us just for nothing.

I don't know what to do are where to turn to. My mother and father took me and my kids in. We had no money to spend, I put all my trust, my hopes and dreams in the Lord, a stream line of blessing came rolling in. My sister took us in too, every day she preaching at me too. Suddenly a light bulb comes on and the explanation is so clear, I was so thankful of them being so dear.

I love this person so dearly; he can't even come near me. He brightens my day when he calls, girl stop worrying he will do it all. Even though he is always busy, he do makes the time to mess me. But at the end he always seems to come through, talking about its ok girl God got you. You think you know me, but I get down on my knees just to pray for you and your kids. We discuss the issue about the land, girl drop everything and put it in God's hands. My very own planters I agree, God thank you for making him like me.

My other shock on top of that was the losing of my job after all of that. Working there for four years, being denied for unemployment for 3 months brought me in tears. Going day by day without a check, I don't know where to turn to I was a wreck. I work a temp job for a week and God bless me with 300 dollars that came in from a leak. We was able to contribute with that blessing, I hope you are getting a great listen.

I cry for help but no one could hear me. Because I hold it in so no one could see. A church member came and say what will it be, or you going to let me try and to be the one that can possibly help you. She made many calls, day and night, please don't hesitate I'm hope I'm right. God will bring you through the light, me and your mother pray for you with all our might. Don't give up you got a great bite, you are a strong young lady it's that right.

I sold my living room suit and my dinette set, to get my children some school clothes that were my only bet. We sold it to someone in need; they had a nice place to put it indeed. I'm having problems with my truck still no answer. I still don't have a place to stay. God please take these problems away. I sat down and listen to myself complain as I do the same things over and over again for who is to blame. I got a high school diploma, a business diploma, and certificates in Word Processing. Don't forget the writing for Magazines Diploma progress.

I got an incredible imagination for writing; just give me a pen and paper you got me like lightening. I can draw anything I want. I'm a multi-talented person, and I still don't have a clue. God bless me with this how about you?

I've been call smiley for the season; I can keep a smile for any reason. I can keep a smile on my face, and hold it good with a case. A beautiful smile they may say, it is tearing me inside day by day. I got on my knees to pray, Lord help me in this trying delay.

All of these leads to the one and only why my life is changing and I are getting the clue that I got to go through what I'm going through. I'm realizing now that I have to pray until something happens. Not prayer on my bad days but on my good days to. I'm a total wreck inside. I'm depressed, sick, and broke but I manage to keep this false smile upon my face. I'm remembering the pastor words it's not about you, or about me it's about God do you believe that's true. Every time he sees me, the only words he says is keep smiling you know God got you.

I thought about it and I can pray any place and any time. I don't have to be ashamed to because God is always on time...

Now I know after all "I can't hide it" but it was Jesus who help me through it. My body and my kids are doing a lot better, this entire loving people that care for me. We are not in my house; I guess you figure that out. It' was my mother who said you better get out, she pray and pray over the house, get out you devil and leave them about. I'm back drawing and writing short stories which I know is going to get publish soon. I have a stronger fate which I couldn't presume.

I'm going to stop making the wrong mistakes over and over again, but I still don't have a place to stay, but I know in my heart as long as I pray until something happens it will happen one day. The stranger I've became to myself is coming out, and God is the one who is going to bring me out. I want to thank God for all he has done for me and my family and others we won.

I want to thank God for giving me a mind, to think and write it was so kind. I want to thank God for making away for me and my kids, and I know a home is coming for us it is. I want to thank God for life itself. I want to thank God for everything, and I know he is about to come in my life and make some extraordinary changes and you know what "I Can't Hide It."

NO ONE WOULD LISTEN

WRITTEN BY: AMANDA JONES

Smileyjonesbooks.info

NO ONE WOULD LISTEN

I was so upset when I first found out what it was, but to have so many people tell you that they can't help you when that is what they are here for to help you. I'm 34 years old single mother with two kids. I have an 8 year old son and a 12 year old daughter. We found black toxic mold in our home called Stachboytrus. Stachboytrus is one of the most dangerous black toxic molds there are.

My kids and I have been having allergies, asthma, sinus, rhinitis, pneumonia, headaches, and unusual sickness for a long time. My son has been hospitalizing numerous of time through to asthma. We have been having these difficulties for years and one day we were cleaning and we notice the bulging walls and wet carpet floors.

That day I went online to locate a mold specialist, because the house smelt musky and the things we were finding was shocking. I should have known something was wrong the whole house was carpet all the way through except the kitchen. I have been leaving here for 8 years and I have repair floors and walls more than twice. I had to repair the laundry room and didn't even have a washer and dryer and couldn't figure out where the water was coming from.

I pull the carpet up in the laundry room and there was black roofing shingles under the carpet. I was very shock because under that was rotten tile and under that was wet plywood and visibility to the ground.

Despite of the laundry room wetness all under these were did it come from? The back door was leaking water inside of the house and also into the side from the roof. The walls were always sweating throughout the house which still didn't ring a bell to me. I have gotten the laundry room repair two times before I even was able to purchase a washer and dryer for that area. All around the walls trimming up and down was wet and nasty looking.

I notice my son room was next door so I pull up carpet in there as well and what did you know. My son whole room was wet under the carpet under the old tile and the wet plywood.

My son room was terrible and he had to stop sleeping in there long before this was found because he said he can't breathe when he is in there. His wall was wet which connect to the laundry room and the kitchen. I have repaired his room three times, and at this time when his Asthma was discovered.

I already saw the bulging walls in my living room behind my television, by my front door, and the whole in the floor at the front door. There was never any gutters place on the house only water running down into the side of the door, which the door is made for a house not a mobile home. My bathroom floor is caving in and my closet has a nice size mold spot just staring me in the face when I go in there. I'm afraid to pull up the carpet in my room because I'm afraid of what I will see.

My daughter room is leaking water in from the roof and is afraid to lift her carpet as well. The hallway is caving in and has a big hole in the floor as well as the other bathroom. My kitchen cabinets are fill with mold spots throughout the kitchen and inside it's terrible. I contact environmental consultant to set up an appointment to get an inspection. I paid $225 to get it done and I was right it was mold and plenty of it. It took me a little time to get the money and when I did my report was in.

I had high readings of water moisture in my walls throughout the house because water intrusions was coming in all side of the house and down from the roof. I had high moisture readings and presence of mold throughout my kitchen, laundry room, son's room, hallway, second bathroom, daughter's room, living room, my bedroom, my closet, and my bathroom.

Mold presence is on the front door and on the outside of the house and all around it. Mold is on top of the house where there is a cap with holes around it. I thought caps go on top double wide when they put them together no single wide. All of this water has been coming in all throughout the house, and under the house mold is growing on the ground.

I report these to the insurance company when I got the report back and it took them nearly 2 weeks before they would come out. They took pictures and inspect and considered everything a Maintenance issue. I'm still stuck on that because:

- I never knew you suppose to cut the carpet up off the floor when you buy your home to look for mold, water, and wetness moisture on the floors.

- I never knew you suppose to take the sheetrock down off the walls to see if there is wet mold growing in the walls of the home.

-I never knew you suppose to climb on top of your house to see if they accidently patch a cap up there to cover ongoing holes that weren't fixing but patch up.

-I never knew you suppose to crawl under the house your buying to see if it's wet under the bottom and see if mold presence.

Who does those things when there buying a home?

 I contact Mortgage company as well and told them the mold issue, fax them the report, and the only thing they could say was when I was going to make another payment and to call the sales center . I call them several times and discuss it with them but the sales manager told me if you were on the side of the road with a flat tire isn't you going to fix your tire? Oh well fix your home.

My environmental consultant said the house was unsafe for us to live in and that we need to move out right away. My house can kill us is all I could think of. I got me and my kids out the same day leaving everything behind. We didn't have anything but the clothes that was on our back.

My mother and father took me and my kids in for six months. Throughout these six months have tried to contact every possible agency, community action, departments, businesses and all and no one could help us. A couple of places want to put us in a shelter because they thought we were batter of domestic violence? Still no one would listen are help us. I file bankruptcy and lost my job as well doing these time period.

My life couldn't get any worse than it has been. I felt like just given up but my mother talking with me just about every night, Mrs. Barbara talking with me at any time I needed, and the pastor prayers and telling me to pray until something happen. They made me stronger everyday as I struggle through these hard times.

One day the mortgage company calls and is interest in fixing the home as it made my kids and me really happy. My prayers have been answer I proclaim and boasted. It wasn't a full week later and they told my bankruptcy lawyer to tell me that my home is unfixable and they wanted me to voluntarily surrender the home and my land to them as a repression because I was the blame for the mold.

Two days before Thanksgiving this is the type of call I get that I got a week to make a decision before the remove the home and take my land as well. I just started crying and couldn't figure out what these people were thinking. I have call lawyers that don't take this kind of cases but now I'm contacting the news people and let them decide what kind of people could put a single mother and two kids out on the streets just because they want to patch up my home and resale it to someone else to make them sick and not know anything about what is going on here. The news people couldn't help, I hope I don't melt.

I'm going to pray until something happen and hope someone can hear me and help us because No One Would Listen.

Smileyjonesbooks.info

Made in the USA
Charleston, SC
25 April 2012